THE LIFE OF A

Lily

Heddie
Thanks for
your support!
Be Blessed +
Highly Favored!
J Kathy
2008

Heidi!

Thanks for
your support +
the fabulous flowers
Lots of love
xxx

THE LIFE OF A
Lily

Growing in His Strength, Blooming in His Love

LILY L. RATLIFF

Tate Publishing *& Enterprises*

The Life of a Lily
Copyright © 2007 by Lily L. Ratliff. All rights reserved.

This title is also available as a Tate Out Loud product. Visit www.tatepublishing.com for more information.

No part of this publication may be reproduced, stored in a retrieval system or transmitted in any way by any means, electronic, mechanical, photocopy, recording or otherwise without the prior permission of the author except as provided by USA copyright law.

Unless otherwise marked, all Scripture quotations are taken from the *Holy Bible, King James Version*, Cambridge, 1769. Used by permission. All rights reserved.

The opinions expressed by the author are not necessarily those of Tate Publishing, LLC.

Published by Tate Publishing & Enterprises, LLC
127 E. Trade Center Terrace | Mustang, Oklahoma 73064 USA
1.888.361.9473 | www.tatepublishing.com

Tate Publishing is committed to excellence in the publishing industry. The company reflects the philosophy established by the founders, based on Psalm 68:11,
"The Lord gave the word and great was the company of those who published it."

Book design copyright © 2007 by Tate Publishing, LLC. All rights reserved.
Cover design by Elizabeth A. Mason
Interior design by Lindsay B. Behrens

Published in the United States of America

ISBN: 978-1-60462-228-7
1. Biography & Autobiography   2. Personal Memoirs/Religious
07.12.28

DEDICATION

To my Lord and Savior, Jesus Christ, who not only saved me, but also called me for such a time as this. I thank you for giving me the vision to write this book. Never would I have imagined this. Because of you, lives will be changed. I love you, Lord!

    To all of my family. I am who I am because of you. I love you dearly. To a great friend of the family Connie, for your inspiration, advice, and encouragement in all of my transitions. You are beautiful in every way.

    To my daughter: Asia Denise Ratliff, who is truly a blessing to me. You have grown to be such a beautiful little girl. God has and will always bless and keep you. Remember you are fearfully and wonderfully made. I love you and don't you ever forget that.

There are friends that I've known for more than ten years who have stuck by me through thick and thin: Keisha and Nathaniel Mitchell, Shelly Clark, and Jermaine Brown. Then there are new friends that have come into my life: Elaine Hamilton (sorority sister) and Sharon SeaBrooks–Jackson (the Godmother of my baby girl). For all of those whom I have passed along the way to shape me in to whom I have so far become, whether positively or negatively, thank you. I have learned so much.

I need to give a shout out to all of my sorority sisters of Zeta Phi Beta Sorority, Inc., especially the Nu Upsilon Zeta Chapter of Temple Terrace, Florida. Thank you for being my sisters and for encouraging me to step out on faith. You all are the best! To my captivating brothers of Phi Beta Sigma Fraternity, Inc. for the bond that we share. It will never fade away. Blue–Phi!

To all of the students I have ever taught in Hillsborough County, Florida, you will forever mean the world to me.

Finally, this is dedicated to my brother, the late Maurice Jamison Hooker, Sr. This book meant even more to me because *our* story needs to be heard! Let it never die. I miss you and love you! May you rest in perfect peace. "Po Child Cup."

TABLE OF CONTENTS

Giving Birth Ain't Easy

13

Never Burn Your Bridges;
They May Start Crumbling Down

17

Can the Real Dead–Beat Dad
Please Stand Up?

21

As I Look in the Mirror,
What Reflection Do I See?

25

Mommy Dearest

33

My Mother, My Best Friend

39

Training up a Child
Is So Hard to Do

45

Where Did I Go Wrong?
I Wasn't Raised This Way

53

Thank God for Saving Me

63

A Gift Only God Can Give

67

Uncovered and Not Ashamed

75

The Devil Sure Knows How to
Be Busy in My Business

83

Fallen but Not Defeated

95

When You Think All is Said and Done,
Look What God Can Do

117

PREFACE

I have come to a point in my life when it's time to look back and remember the good times and bad, my ups and downs, my past, present, and ultimate turn to the future. Why has it come to a point in which to write this book? For me, it's a time of reflection; my experiences have been ones that demanded a step–back–and–take–notice approach—"Hey you, wake up!" so to speak. Have I always been good? By no means. Have I ever sinned and wished I could take those times back? Many times, but I can't. However, God has forgiven me and now I can only pray and hope that God will continue to shine his light of love, hope, and security upon me. I've been blessed in so many ways, but I had to go through many things to get to where I am now. I have not arrived. I only dare to dream of the possibilities.

This book is for women and men who have ever hurt or been hurt, abused, battered, talked about, or emotionally and physically drained, as well as for the countless number of children who, for some reason or another, have given up hope about ever being loved and wanted in this world. I've been there many times, but I hope that through my testimony, you will realize, you will be shaken, and you will even be determined in your spirit to act. I trust that as you read these words of encouragement, you too will "wake up" and see the salvation of the Lord.

> Lord, grant me the wisdom to recognize Satan for who he is. He has attempted to destroy many people's lives, and has unfortunately succeeded. But I pray, in the name of Jesus, that from this day forward, as my fellow brothers and sisters take notice of the devil's tactics through reading this book, their lives will be transformed and uplifted. Amen.

This is *The Life of a Lily.*

GIVING BIRTH AIN'T EASY

My parents were people who have gone through a great deal in their lives. My mother, twenty-one years of age at my birth, just years before graduated from high school and was searching for many opportunities when she came across my father. He was handsome, light-skinned, had very curly hair and a look that would turn any woman upside down just gazing at him. Born outside of Kingston in St. Andrew, Jamaica, he was sowing his royal oats by coming to the United States. Upon moving to Kissimmee, Florida, he met my mother, had a brief courtship, and ended up marrying her. He only had one problem—he didn't know how to treat a woman.

Domestic violence: It can be a deadly disease if not treated. Why do I say disease? Because it plays on the mind and one's emotions. Being physically or mentally abused, or both, can lead to serious consequences, even death, and also can be a by-product of future generations. Satan does everything he can to destroy marriages and homes. If not rebuked in the heavenly realm, it can trickle down to your children, watching what daddy did to mommy. "The thief cometh not, but for to steal, and to kill, and to destroy" (John 10:10, KJV). Children may grow up to think that it's okay to do it to my wife or my husband and/or children. And believe it or not, many women commit domestic disputes, just like men. The numbers are on the rise.

I was told that during my parents' marriage, good and bad times occurred, but more bad times infiltrated the marriage than pleasant ones. Infidelity and emotional and verbal abuse kept times with them at an all-time low. My mother became pregnant with me at a time when things between them couldn't have been worse. My father would come home from work to always find the same man sitting on the front porch. My mom insisted that he was just a friend and needed a place to stay for a little while, but it became more and more apparent of the real reason why he was constantly there. So my father left for a while. When he came back a short time later, policemen were staked out around the whole house. Reportedly, my father had a .22–caliber handgun and was going to "shoot the baby out of her belly." With all of the chaos that was happening between them, he decided that it was time for him to leave. Meanwhile, my mother became very ill. She wouldn't eat and became very depressed.

On April 25, 1974, I was born in Orlando, Florida, at Orlando Regional Medical Center. Three pounds, seven ounces, so my mother says. I was told that I slept in a small shoebox and sometimes a Chek drinking box. I was small enough to hold in the palm of a hand.

Being brought home already premature and malnourished, my mother still found a way not to feed me. She would give baby food away to other people's babies, half feed me, and hide food from my grandmother to make it look like I was fed. My mother was going through some serious emotional trauma from the breakup between her and my father. When they found out my health was not improving, my grandparents persuaded my mom to let me live with them.

My grandparents were very active in my life at the time. After a while of being taken care of by my grandparents, I was taken to the doctor to find out that I had a bad case of tuberculosis, which is a swelling in the lungs or joints that is caused by a bacterium called tubercles. The only thing the doctors could tell my grandparents to do was to take me home, make me feel loved, and, in so many words, watch me die. But my grandmother believed in the power of prayer. She prayed the prayer of faith and laid me on her stomach when she slept, so that I could learn to breathe by feeling the way she breathed. Within days the Lord healed my body. Doctors were amazed at the progress. From that day on, life would never be the same between my mom and my grandparents.

NEVER BURN YOUR BRIDGES; THEY MAY START CRUMBLING DOWN

Only being a few months old and having suffered and healed from a potentially fatal ailment, my grandparents decided to adopt me. These are grandparents who have two grown children of their own, both of which my grandfather decided to adopt after marrying my grandmother. I guess it was still in his blood to take in another little one to love and care for, but I for one didn't see them as my adopted parents or even my grandparents. From a young age, they were known as my mama and daddy. I think my biological mom resented that so much that she attempted to take me back when my "parents" weren't around.

She did this one day while my great-grandmother kept me when my grandparents were at work. My biological mom was living in Orlando at the time. She knew where I was and what time I was going to be picked up, so she came to Kissimmee and took me from my great-grandmother with a struggle. Nonetheless, she carried out what she wanted to do. Immediately, my great-grandmother called my grandfather from work telling him what happened. What my grandparents didn't know at the time was that my biological mother wanted to take me and give me to her then-mother-in-law so that she could collect food stamps and the Women, Infants, and Children program because she had me. Plus, that would give her mother-in-law a chance to get a check on the first and fifteenth of each month. Well, whatever reason she had for doing what she did, it was not acceptable—especially to my "daddy."

On his way to Orlando to retrieve me, my grandfather brought along with him a sawed-off shotgun. He was ready to go to jail for his "little girl." It just took one look at my grandfather with that gun to let everyone know he meant business. Bursting through the house in Orlando, he held the gun in one hand and took me in the other. He pointed the gun at my biological mother and told her that the next time she tried to steal "the baby," he would kill her. Never again were there any problems, but it damaged the family for quite some time.

CAN THE REAL DEAD-BEAT DAD PLEASE STAND UP?

My biological father has been in and out of my life ever since I was born. My father is the age of fifty-seven now, and he has probably played Santa five or six times in my life. Each time, he has tried to prove himself around my grandparents by giving me money and lavish presents and trying to take me around to see other family members or friends to introduce me as "his daughter." While I was once an outcast, by age nine I was finally worth loving. Maybe I started to look like him. Why am I saying all this, you may ask? Because as a little girl, my grandmother told me stories about why I was adopted. The only thing the stories did was fuel up negative energy toward my father. Year after year, many different holidays and birthdays came, and I waited to be able to see him walk through the door, but he didn't show. So of course, after a while, I would go on with life, knowing he would not be a part of it. This would go on for years in a row, until he would show up again years later with the same routine. I constantly felt abandoned and neglected. You can see how feeling this way can put a damper on your social life. Ultimately, your past feelings of neglect will rise up in every future relationship you try to have . To conquer it, you would have to undergo deliverance from it, asking God to restore you and your past, which God will so graciously do if you just ask and receive the salvation of the Lord.

Unfortunately, I didn't see it that way for years. Up until the age of thirteen, I was lost, having very low self-esteem and feeling timid, feeble, sickly, and constantly thought of as one who was hanging on by a string. No one, including my father, thought I would make anything of myself; I would be dead before I'd even get out of grade school. From the time my grandmother first told me about my being adopted, I automatically assumed that no one loved me or wanted me around. If it had not been for the Lord watching over me, I would have either been dead or sent around to every foster or orphanage home known to man. I really feel God equipped my grandparents with the task of caring for me, no matter what the price. Because of that, it really didn't matter to me whether I had my biological father in my life or not.

AS I LOOK IN THE MIRROR, WHAT REFLECTION DO I SEE?

As I've been growing up, I've been trying to find out what mannerisms and appearances I get from my biological parents. If your parents have raised you all your life, things like this may not concern you. However, when you've been adopted or given to foster care, not ever knowing who your parents were or look like, you may at one time or another want to know. Yes, I saw my biological parents off and on during my childhood, but didn't know much about them as far as their personality, such as how they reacted to things. While learning bits and pieces about them, I've come to find out several things. First, I do look much more like my mother: her acne–prone, caramel complexion, the same hands and feet and pointy chin, and when I give certain looks to people, I hear people tell me, "You know, you really look like your mother." As far as my father, I've inherited his thick, wavy-to-curly hair and many of his mannerisms. However, I've also inherited his stubbornness and bad temper, which have tampered my life. I'm not saying those traits are bad. In many cases it has helped me get where I am today in my career, and achieve success because I am persistent and extremely aggressive in my plans and aspirations. My sorority sisters nicknamed me Intensity, and I feel it fits me perfectly. They truly find me to have a drive and a zealous ambition in all aspects of what I do. I will give until I can't give anymore and it's often difficult for me to say no. On the reverse side of this, these traits have negatively affected me because my stubbornness and aggression have influenced many of my relationships, not only my marriage, but my family, especially with my biological parents. When you have inherited much of your personality from your parents, they and only they know how to handle you because you are so much like them.

My mother and I battled for years for the attention of my grandmother. We both loved her dearly and were spoiled, but because I was adopted by my grandmother, that put me in the forefront in regards to a lot of issues. I was younger and couldn't take care of myself, let alone defend myself, so I was treated differently, given things that my mother never received, and excused from doing chores. I had to do none of those things because I was considered the only child since I hadn't been living with or raised with my brother. My mother resented this and would say sly things to my mom in front of me so that I would know that I was getting away with a lot of things. If I got new clothes, she felt she needed to have them too, or if I was given a car, my mother was angry because I didn't do anything to deserve it. It hurt me very much to hear the woman who birthed me saying these kinds of things. Children in the neighborhood who wanted to hang out with me didn't because my mom would say things to make parents feel that I was a bad influence on their children. How could I be? I was a loner and isolated at home. I never went out or hung out on the corner. I hardly had friends over or was allowed to stay at their houses. Mama and Daddy were strict. As I look back, I'm glad and understand why. When I go back home now as an adult and see all of the people that I went to school with, they are either pregnant, have three or four babies already, or are in jail. They don't have college degrees and some didn't finish high school. I thank God for how I was raised.

My relationship with my mother became so bad; she even stooped low enough to accuse my grandfather of sexually abusing me. One day, she and her then husband came over telling my grandmother things that were total untruths. She said things like, "I believe Daddy has been touching Lily and messing with her." When my granddad and I got wind of it, we were both floored with anger and disbelief. I found out one night when my grandmother came into my room as I was listening to music. She told me to take off my headphones because she needed to ask me something. Then she asked me a question I thought I would never have to hear from someone who truly loved and trusted me. She asked if daddy had ever touched or done something to me. I looked at her with disbelief and puzzlement as to why she felt this way. Of course, I told her no. I explained that I was usually in one room listening to music or watching MTV, and he was usually in the other room watching some football game or his favorite television show. I was isolated. We didn't bother each other, but if I really needed something, he was there. After our talk, my grandmother left the room, of course trusting my response, but she still went to him to discuss it. And behind closed doors, I could imagine the feeling she must have had. I was her baby. And even though she loved him from the very beginning, I had a special place in her heart, which she did not want destroyed.

Finally the day came when my mother and her estranged husband came back over to continue the alleged rumors and tell about signs that they thought they had seen to prove of my granddad's inappropriate behavior. It got so bad that my grandmother all of a sudden slumped over in her seat and onto the floor. I immediately knew something was wrong, but for some reason, everybody was just standing there either in disbelief or not realizing that she was having a heart attack. I did what I thought was the best and rapid response any child would do, which was to call 911. I believe she was heartbroken that my mother would cause such a scene for the attention and love of someone. Even though my grandmother came through this and the prognosis was a positive one, it worsened the ties between her and my mother for some time.

On another occasion, as time passed, I will never forget my mother telling my grandmother, in front of me, that she wouldn't help me go to college and that I better get out and get a job like she did so I could work and pay for it on my own. Sometimes that baffles me still today. Why wouldn't she want to see me succeed? Why would she want me to work some of the same meaningless jobs that she and so many others work—regular nine-to-five, minimum-wage work that only got you by while you work paycheck to paycheck to cover expenses? I wanted much more for myself, and so did my grandmother. She was extremely proud of me, even up to the time of her passing. But I wanted that feeling to also rest on my mother. Even though she didn't raise me, I wanted her to feel proud in her heart for the accomplishments I made and that my grandparents took over the reigns to raise me correctly. I would have been okay and felt a little better toward her had she felt those things, but instead I had a greater rage and feeling of rejection and started to question my existence. My relationship with my mother left a bitter taste in my mouth that I knew only God himself could change.

MOMMY DEAREST

My grandmother, Mrs. Doretha (Brown) Hooker, was born on March 11, 1937, to Lillie Mae Brown, after whom I was named, and Norman Brown, in Rock Hill, South Carolina. This was a woman who was truly real. Growing up during the Forties and Fifties wasn't always easy. She had to defend herself many times in school. I remember sitting in a Wendy's restaurant with her, eating while listening to her tell me about a time when she had to hit a girl with a brick to keep the girl from jumping on her for a second time. Mama, as I called her, always taught me to stand my ground, but that wasn't me. During that mother–daughter talk in Wendy's, my twelve-year-old frame of mind still had me thinking that I would never want to lay a hand on anyone. If anything, I just wanted people to like me since I was such an attention-seeker at the time. My four-foot-eleven-inch, eighty-five-pound frame was finally gaining enough sustenance to start to show a little weight, even though I still looked straight up and down with no hips or breasts; but Mama didn't see it that way.

During the time she was on the earth, I didn't know her to have very many friends, but she always felt it was better that way. Looking back, I feel that no one ever really had the chance to see her for who she really was. Even though she only had an eleventh-grade education, her sense of self and overall character truly outshined and was beyond her years. She had such wisdom and common sense and a style about her that I think she passed on to me. She felt that even though we didn't have all the money in the world didn't mean we had to dress that way. She went out and made sure that we had the best of everything. Was I spoiled? Maybe. But at the same time, she taught me how to save. She was also very particular about what I wore and how my hair was done. She was definitely a believer that a woman's hair is a glory to her. She never wanted me to cut or even trim my hair. Maybe that was because as a baby I had to have little bows taped on my head to show that I was a girl. So Mama moisturized, brushed, and groomed it until it grew long. She was therefore very protective of my hair, as if it were her own.

I remember her waking me up early on a Saturday, trying to sneak us out of the house without Daddy (my grandfather) knowing to go to breakfast together and talk about many different things—life, relationships, the Bible, and her experiences as a child—all of which helped me see my own life and future. Then we would go shopping, and that's when I understood about style and fashion. Dooney and Bourke, Etienne Aigner, you name it, I had it. I'll admit; it rolled over for me into adulthood. I don't see myself as high maintenance, but I do like nice things and strive to get them. But what made me love her, as well as my grandfather, so much more was the fact that she did everything to make sure I had what I wanted, even if they had to forego things for themselves. From choir robes for the church choir to costumes and money for weekend trips with the school chorus, I had it because they saw something in me, which others couldn't or didn't want to see—a drive and ambition to succeed. Because of that, I thank them today.

I remember my grandmother always telling people, "You know Lily is different. Don't fault her because she's that way." I never really understood what she meant by that, but now I think I do. I think she said that because I was considered an only child in the eyes of so many people, even though I had a younger half-brother that I was not raised with on my biological mother's side. I was spoiled, never had to do much of anything, and was much different than the rest of the family, and I think she kind of conditioned me that way. She looked at me very highly and treated me as such by the way she dressed me, kept me in the church, and instilled in me great morals and what she called "future mother wit and common sense." And because of that, even when I was around other family members at gatherings, I could tell I was treated and perceived differently, and when I would come around, conversations would change—even in their language and tone of voice. It seemed as though they were saying, "There's Lily. We better not say that." In many ways, this made me feel like an outcast. It was bad enough that I felt like I was not wanted by my biological parents and pawned off to be taken care of by my grandparents. But don't get me wrong; if it had not been for them, I don't know where I would be now. I'm blessed more for being raised appropriately by them, and I've come so far now. Looking back, I understand these things.

She also never wanted my family to tell me when there was any bad news. From the time she lived even until now, my family would have a hard time calling or telling me anything that would be hurtful. Whether someone in the family was sick or in the hospital, she told them that she didn't want me to worry because she knew how fragile, emotional, and overwhelmed I could be about things. So the family would consider her request by not telling me about negative circumstances in order to keep me calm and focused on my studies while I was in school.

Throughout her lifetime, which was up to my being twenty-five years of age, she always told me that she wanted me to be better than she was. She wanted me to be independent enough to not need a man to take care of me. She always knew I wanted to be a teacher, so she would go around and make sure everyone knew I was going to be one. I believe she was very proud of me—not necessarily for the person I was, but for the person she knew I would become.

MY MOTHER, MY BEST FRIEND

Before her passing in 1999 from cancer, I sat down with my mom and made a promise. She really wanted me to go and get my master's degree. I had already finished college at the time for my bachelor's degree in English education from the University of South Florida in Tampa, but she knew as well as I did that I had more to do. My mom, for as long as I can remember, had worked as a "domestic engineer," otherwise known as a housekeeper. She wanted more for me and didn't want me to follow in the footsteps of her, nor my biological mom, who was also in the business of housekeeping. So we made a pact that I would continue my education. I wanted it badly for myself, but I also had it in my heart to finish my master's degree for her.

Two weeks before I finished my master's, I received a call from my aunt telling me to rush from Tampa to Kissimmee to see Mama. By this time, the cancer had spread from her adrenal gland throughout her body, including her brain cells. Because of this, she developed a type of Alzheimer's disease that caused her to not recognize people or remember where she was. But God made sure that she never lost sight of nor forgot who he was. Hospice volunteers had been coming to see her at home two to three times a week, but that still wasn't enough; she needed around-the-clock care. It had become so bad that one day she was reportedly seen by a neighbor crawling through a window from her room to the outside and sat in the middle of a dirt road covered in ants. Just thinking about it still aches me. This once strong, vibrant, don't-take-nothing-from-nobody sense of a woman had changed to a person that was clinging to all the life she had left and not knowing how desperately alone she was. I remember her talking to me one day while she was in bed. She was laughing, having a good time, and then

THE LIFE OF A LILY

all of a sudden she burst into tears sharing how unloved she felt because no one came to see her, she felt alone in the house, and depression had set in her heart. The doctors had her taking all types of medication for the cancer, even though the doctors knew they had done all that they could do, and she still had to take medications for depression. Many times she wouldn't take it, however, and soon stopped because she knew that depression was really a demon—something that was working against her. Before she became a Christian, when smoking cigarettes and playing Bingo was her way of life, that demon could have easily destroyed her. After becoming saved, though, my mom would fight until the very end. And I believe that she did, even though her memory was starting to fade away.

Two weeks before she passed away, all of the family and I were by her side in the nursing home talking with her and trying to do everything we could do to help her remember the way things used to be. We also tried not to let her feel that we knew God was about to call her home. All of a sudden, for some strange reason, I was compelled to express love—all the love that I've ever felt for this woman in just a matter of seconds. A kiss turned to a parade of loving showers of warmth on my mama's skin. I kissed her across her face, neck, and back over and over telling her, "I love you." Tears ran down the cheeks of my family's faces as if to say one last goodbye wasn't good enough. All the while, my mom smiled like she would if she recognized someone and, even though the person's name didn't register, she knew she remembered the person's touch or scent. I believe that's all that mattered. When I left, I felt a sense of pain, but acceptance for what was to happen. I got tired of seeing her suffer such a long hardship and excruciating pain from cancer. Praying and crying out for God's will was all that mattered to me. Even though I was going through a terrible divorce from my first husband at the same time, all of that lay on the backburner as I waited in silence.

October 1, 1999, at 8:05 p.m., my friend and mother left this world behind. She was sixty-two years old. When I received the call later that night,

I fell to my knees in agony not because I didn't know it was coming; I had accepted God's will for her. The person that I knew would always be there when I needed someone would not be on the other end of the phone anymore. She was my best friend. She taught me so many valuable lessons about life, about being myself, and about making something of myself. God truly blessed me by bringing us together. She helped to truly shape me into the woman I am today. I miss her dearly, but one day we will meet again, "In the sweet by and by."

TRAINING UP A CHILD IS SO HARD TO DO

"Train up a child in the way that *she* should go: and when *she* gets old, *she* will not depart from it" (Proverbs 22:6, my italics and gender changes). This Scripture helped me to see circumstances in two different ways: First, I realized that my parents' trained me up old school with loving wisdom and street smarts, strict discipline, and high ethical, moral, and spiritual standards. And second, they trained up a child going from one stage of education to another, not forgetting to acknowledge all of the trials, mishaps, and experiences along the way. I realized that as I was a child, my parents really raised me up to understand everything that was needed to live a responsible and productive life. Yes, they were strict, and they had tough love through much of my childhood, but all of it I remember and cherish dearly.

During my teenage years, I grew up surrounded by love, but strict discipline, as well. I didn't always get away with things that other children would. Teenage pregnancy was something my parents would never have to worry about; I was too scared to kiss a boy, let alone have sex. And on top of that, I was too scared of what my parents would do to me if they found out! I received the gift of salvation at the age of thirteen, so my mind was far from doing things that disrespected myself or God or shamed my parents. I went on through school focusing on my studies and being involved in my church.

When becoming saved at thirteen, I had a spiritual father in my pastor. He was a pastor who catered to all constituents, both young and old. He made the word of God understandable to everyone, which helped me study God's word, pray, and ultimately get closer to God in an intimate way. I would love to sing a solo in the church choir during his leadership because he felt I had an anointing, and others saw it too. Under his administration, many new members and converts came to Christ. The church would be packed every week and the choir had an anointing that blessed many hearts. When the church let him go because of matters I still don't understand, it seemed like a piece of me went with him. By no means did we see him as God, but we truly saw God in him. As a result, I slowly moved away from an interest in the church and I felt that every other pastor that came and went wasn't good enough.

By the age of fifteen, my eyes turned to more worldly endeavors—boys. I feel that if my eyes and heart were still on God like they should have been, my mind for boys would not have been so easy for me to conjure up. During that period up to age eighteen, I had a few boyfriends—four to be exact—and I had stopped going to church almost altogether. My relationships consisted of talking on the phone, kissing, holding hands, maybe visiting their parents, but for the most part, were very structured. My parents still had a hold of what I was to do. Most of the relationships lasted no more than three to six months. It wasn't until almost my eighteenth birthday and being a senior in high school that those seemingly miniscule relationships went to another level. I had met the one. He was three years my junior, and he was fine, Puerto Rican, and a great dresser. He wooed me and made me want to take the word "relationship" to the next step. *All of my friends have had sex before,* I would think. They would even go as far as to tell me about their recent encounters. I was the only senior, it seemed, that was still a virgin. So, after several encounters, love letters, and late-night phone calls to my sweetheart, we succumbed to a night of fornication. "He that committeth fornication sinneth against his own body" (I Corinthians 6:18). We didn't know what we were doing, but we were grown and in love; or at least I thought I was. Little did I know at the time that I was a small child inside crying for attention and someone to love me. Even though my grandparents took good care of me, I still felt distanced because many times I stayed in my room alone.

THE LIFE OF A LILY

No one thought about just talking, giving a hug, or going for a family outing.

My first love lasted about six months, which was a long time for me back then. We broke up when I went off to college. We didn't want to, but we knew a long-distance relationship wouldn't work. Two weeks after I graduated from high school, I went off to college to the University of South Florida, in Tampa Bay. Many kids go off to college and cry from being homesick. But for me, I thought it was a sign of freedom, being a grown up and finally able to make my own decisions. Most of all, I was happy that I got the chance to scope out men. What I didn't know was that freshman girls like myself were being scoped out as "fresh meat" by upperclassmen. They think about which girls they can sleep with first. Forget about a relationship—it's a matter of what men call, "sticking and moving" on to the next girl. I was so naïve that I had to get to know the first handsome man I saw, who happened to be in a fraternity. Unfortunately, our intentions were very conflicting.

One night, three guys came to my dorm room to see me. I was already dressed for bed, but was only expecting to see one of them, Jeremy. I thought they were only going to be there for a few minutes, so I let them in. Minutes after they came in, all of them went into the hallway to talk. Seconds later, Jeremy came back in alone. He sat on the bed next to me and stared me down. I didn't think he would try anything, but I was wrong. He started kissing me and told me he wanted me. My intentions led me to believe that he wanted to be with me as my boyfriend. His only intention was to have sex with me. All I remember was doing things I didn't like, but not one time did I stop him. Deep down inside, I thought he liked me and I would be able to see him again. It lasted maybe twenty minutes before he quickly left. I felt violated by Jeremy and hated and disgraced by dorm mates as he walked out and I came out behind him still in my nightclothes. Girls started talking; I was called names. *I am not all those things they say,* I thought. My encounter with him got around so quickly that the whole co-ed dorm knew about it by the next morning. All I could do was cry. As a result, I stayed secluded for a whole month, hardly went to class, and didn't hang out much. I sought counseling, but depression nearly ate me alive. When campus officials found out what happened, they suspended him for two years. He couldn't step back on campus. Sometimes I wonder if what occurred to me ever happened to someone else. Had he already been in a similar situation and was finally given this punishment after realizing his non–compliance to university standards? But at that time, this didn't matter to me; I was still the laughing stock of the whole black student body. Sororities wouldn't take me into their pledging process because of what they heard. It wasn't until I stood up, faced my fears, and told someone what actually happened that one sorority publicly apologized for its misinformation and lack of professionalism.

As a result of coming out, I became more involved in school activities and even entered a black fraternity beauty pageant in which I won first place. Even though that incident is past me and I've forgiven him for the whole ordeal, my freshman year at USF will not be forgotten. I wish many of the students there could see me now. Isn't it funny how God can turn messes into miracles? He has a great sense of humor!

WHERE DID I GO WRONG?
I WASN'T RAISED THIS WAY

While I was in college, I met my first husband. I met him at a club on a night that I really was not planning to go out. However, some girls I hung out with at the time talked me into going, and the rest was history. I was nineteen; he had just turned twenty–three. We talked, exchanged numbers, went out on a couple of dates and just considered ourselves a couple from that point on. That lasted six on–and–off–again years of emotions, confusion, and tension. It was the kind of love where you are out of touch with yourself, your defenses are down, you are love struck, filled with drama, and jealous all at once. I didn't get along with his mother, either. In fact, she didn't want us dating because I was so young, but we continued to do our thing.

By the time I turned twenty, I was living with him and completely left the college dormitory and the activities that come with being a student. I was so out of touch because I wanted to be with him. My parents were hurt—especially my grandmother. I knew she didn't raise me that way. We didn't speak for months. When she did call, she would speak to him to see how I was doing. All of a sudden, he wanted to go out with his boys and wouldn't call or come home until 5 a.m. Not feeling like we were truly being honest with each other, I started to do the same. But when I did, he found that offensive and kicked me out of the apartment. My family had to come all the way there to help me move out. For a whole week I had to stay with a girlfriend of mine and pay her daily so that I would not be without food or shelter. Then I would go back to him, even after he told my family that he just wanted some space. How stupid could I be? I could hear my mom telling me, "I told you so. You know you shouldn't have moved out of the dorm. Always have somewhere to go in case a man wants his space. That way you'll always have yours." Boy, have I learned over the years. Anyway, this went back and forth for four long years. Why did I go through all this drama? I felt he was all I had. Many women feel that way. You are with someone for so long and you've given everything you have; you'd rather stay where you've expended all of your energy. After four years of this, we decided to get married. We had a small ceremony back home in Kissimmee. Unfortunately, during our marriage, I finally learned that he wasn't what God would have for me. The Bible says, "Be ye not unequally yoked together with unbelievers: for what fellowship hath righteousness with unrighteousness? And what communion hath light with darkness?" (II Corinthians 6:14)

The first year of marriage seemed to have gone well. We bought our first home and I thought we had put the past behind us. We tried having a family for a year and a half. We had several tests and surgeries done through an infertility specialist. I found out that I might never have children unless I went through a serious medical procedure to correct blocked fallopian tubes. Even though this hurt me and made me feel like I wasn't a woman because I couldn't have children, he became more rebellious and angry. So to fulfill his desires, he started going out again. He even told me, "Don't worry about it. I'll just get another woman to have my baby." He left me home being a wife and wouldn't come home until early in the morning two to three times a week. Sometimes he would wait until I was asleep and go out. I would wake up in the middle of the night and he would be gone. I'd call him; he wouldn't pick up the phone. What was I to think? I loved him, but I also felt alone and isolated. I felt like I wasn't needed anymore. Our sex life was null and void. We already had difficulties in bed because I was still hung up on emotions stemming from my past incident with Jeremy, so it was difficult for me to make love at the beginning of our relationship. It was hard for him to touch me. I didn't feel clean or sexy, but I didn't want to be alone or without him. I felt he was cheating on me, so for one straight weekend, I stayed out, met someone that I knew for a while from college, and had a one–night stand. It wasn't love or even lust; I just wanted to feel sexy and wanted by someone because I wasn't needed or getting what I needed at home. I was wrong and felt guilty, so I told him what I did. He was floored! He was so upset; I thought he would hurt me. He ripped all of my underwear I had on that day and even hit me like I was a child. I was emotionally drained. I was not Lily anymore. I had no identity. I just wanted to die. In I Corinthians 6:9–10, it says, "Know ye not that the unrighteous shall not inherit the kingdom of God? Be not deceived… neither fornicators…nor adulterers…shall inherit the kingdom of God." I was so glad when I read verse 11: "And such were some of you: but ye are washed, but ye are sanctified, but ye are justified in the name of the Lord Jesus, and by the Spirit of our God". God had something else in mind for me. We stayed together after all of that for another year, when I could no longer take it.

I continued to be a wife, not knowing he was seeing someone else. The emotional and physical abuse worsened. It got to where I couldn't stand to see him and we were even sleeping in separate bedrooms. At that time, I was the only one working, while he went to school to finish his degree. But what I didn't know was that he had met his lover in one of his classes. When I found out he had failed both of his classes, I sat back while watching him lie to his parents, who watched him walk for his graduation when indeed he never really graduated.

I found out what was really going on in my marriage one night when a phone call came in. I had just finished a conference call with my professor because I was working on my master's degree at the time. When the call came in, I saw on the caller ID a name that said Ronnie; I thought it was one of his friends, so I answered the phone. The caller immediately hung up the phone. Seconds later, the phone rang again. This time he rushed to pick it up and went to go into another room with it. As he was talking, I decided to pick up another phone and listen in. Sure enough, it was the voice of a woman, and the nature of the call made me realize I was no longer his number one priority.

It just so happened that I had my bags already packed because I was going to tell him we needed to separate for a time to clear our heads and see if we wanted to continue our marriage or go our separate ways. So when I heard who was now occupying his time, I took my bags and headed toward the front door. With tears in my eyes, I knew I was ready to leave, but I didn't know the first place to go. As I was going to unlock the door, I felt a blow to my head. I had no time to react. I was on the ground and my face was red and bruised. He told me to get up. "Where are you going?" he asked. "You're not going anywhere." We started arguing and, before I knew it, all the anger that I had ever felt toward this man erupted into violence. I started hitting and scratching him. He probably still has scars today. I didn't care anymore. If that meant I had to die in the process for fear he would kill me, then I had to die trying. We were having it out in the living room. As I was trying to get out, he blocked the door, took my bags, and threw them out the front door; all of my stuff went everywhere in the front yard. People in the neighborhood came out of their homes asking me if I was all right. As he was cursing obscenities to me, I packed what I could from the yard and took off until I got to the other side of town. I was so afraid that he was following me; I tried to go somewhere he knew I wouldn't be. I couldn't go home to my family because my parents would call him or he would ride down there. Mind you, he had a licensed gun in his possession and could very well use it. I stopped to a friend's apartment that he didn't know much about and told my friend what happened. My friend called the police and within minutes we were escorted back to my home with seven or eight police deputy cars. I could have easily gone to jail because of the marks that were visible on his chest, but so could he because of the marks he made on my face. A statement was taken, a deputy followed me into the home to get some more of my things, and I left. Now I know why the Lord didn't allow a baby to come into the world at that particular time. God wanted me to have a child, but he wanted it to be with whom he wanted me to be. When I left, I felt a weight was truly lifted off of my shoulders. I went through many obstacles, loneliness, and despair, but God shined his light on me and helped me make it through.

THANK GOD FOR SAVING ME

After I separated from my husband, I thought that everything a marriage was supposed to be just wasn't in my grasp anymore. Even though I knew marriage was a sacred union, one that you don't take lightly, and something you work hard to keep, I had failed at that. I'd come to realize that my marriage of two years was one big lie, a game, and a joke. Neither person in the relationship was innocent by any means, but because flesh was involved, even in the saying of "I do," the devil was ready to destroy it any way he could. He used many evil tactics, including verbal abuse that turned to physical abuse and idleness, which resulted in infidelity. We didn't care for each other; we were both out for our own good. As I said, it was like a game being played and each person was seeing if they could hurt the other enough until ultimately someone won. The time when I finally felt it was time for quits came one early morning before going to work. I decided to go and try to get the rest of my things from our home since I still had a key. As I walked in the door, I heard some noise coming from upstairs. I knew my estranged husband had already gone to work, so what was all the noise? When I got upstairs to our bedroom, I saw something I thought I'd never see: a woman totally naked sitting up in our bed on her cell phone. I immediately started shaking, and my mind was going in all directions. All I could ask was, "How long had this been going on?" "Oh, three times," she replied. Finally it dawned on me that she was Ronnie. She had a look of no remorse, for she knew who I was. Of course, I probably could have shot her dead, but the power of God was all over me. I had just recently re-dedicated my life to Christ, just weeks before my grandmother passed, and I had to think of what was more important: my love for God or for man. I walked out the door without looking back. With this occurrence, I am reminded of the story of Sodom and Gomorrah. The followers of Jesus were warned not to desire their former lives in that city, but Lot's wife "looked back from behind him and turned into a pillar of salt" (Genesis 19:26). Thank you, Jesus, for not letting me look back! Yes, it hurt, but oh the blessings of the Lord that were to follow.

A GIFT ONLY GOD CAN GIVE

> Trust in the Lord, and do good; so shalt thou dwell in the land, and verily thou shalt be fed. Delight thyself also in the Lord; and he shall give the desires of thine heart. Commit thy way unto the Lord; trust also in him; and he shall bring it to pass.
>
> Psalms 37:3–5

I had to go through and experience these things to finally step upon God's gift of salvation, joy, peace, and love. Once I knew who was more important in my life, God began to open doors that no man could close.

While my ex–husband and I were going through our difficult period of emotional and physical abuse with each other, God still helped me to get two degrees: a master's in reading education after the divorce in December 1999 and an education specialist in educational leadership in 2001. I was able to obtain a 3.8 grade point average throughout school. I received a job promotion to Language Arts Department Head at the school where I taught. Then God did a miraculous thing in my life: I received the gift of tongues on November 12, 1999, just a couple of weeks after my grandmother passed away. It happened at an E.C. Reems International Christian Convention that was held at my church. That was a true blessing, one for which I asked the Lord. Days before I had stopped and asked two Holy Spirit–filled women in the church what I needed to do in order to receive this gift. Still pretty much a babe in Christ, I asked them, not knowing that all I had to do was ask God for it. The Lord said, "And whatsoever ye shall ask in my name, that will I do, that the Father may be glorified in the Son. If ye ask anything in my name, I will do it" (John 14:13–14). It also says in John 15:7: "If ye abide in me, and my word abides in you, ye shall ask what ye will, and it shall be done unto you." These are the promises of God. He also said, "Ye have not chosen me, but I have chosen you, and ordained you…whatsoever ye shall ask of the Father in my name, he may give it to you" (John 15:16). So they prayed with me and told me to go home, set the atmosphere, and ask God for what I wanted. I let God handle the rest. That night, on November 12, a turning point in my life occurred. As I was standing up front in the choir stand, the speaker asked us to turn and hold a neighbor's hand and start praying for them. As I started praying, I felt a warm tingle go through my body like you would never believe, and I felt myself go up in the Spirit. I could actually hear myself, but it was an utterance that I'd never heard before. First it sounded like gibberish, as if first learning to speak. Then it sounded like actual words from another language. The Bible says:

> And when the day of Pentecost was fully come, they were all with one accord in one place. And suddenly there came a sound from heaven as of a rushing mighty wind, and it filled all the house where they were sitting. And there appeared unto them cloven tongues like as of fire, and it sat upon

> each of them. And they were all filled with the Holy Ghost, and began to speak with other tongues, as the Spirit gave them utterance.
>
> Acts 2:1–4

I finally returned back to my first love from the age of thirteen, when I had first received the gift of salvation. From that point on, I made sure to talk and confess to God everything that weighed on me. "If we confess our sins, he is faithful and just to forgive us our sins, and to cleanse us from all unrighteousness" (I John 1:9). From that November night, I had an intimacy with the Lord like I've never had before with anyone. My husband, lover, and friend were all wrapped up in Jesus. Instead of coming to Jesus with frivolous requests, I just wanted more of him. When I got off from work, I'd rush home and through the door to him. My new apartment was indeed a sacred haven in which Jesus resided with me. It contained unspeakable peace, love, and joy. I would have dates with Jesus, cooking for my Lord, talking daily with him. I also believe God looked to my heart and spirit and realized I still wanted to be married, so during my time of fellowship with Jesus, the Lord purged and restored me. He showed me myself along the way, faults and all, still loving me enough to teach me how to be a good, godly wife and, ultimately, mother. So I decided to send my petition for a husband to my Lord, specifically telling God my desires. Not only did the Lord hear me, he answered my prayers and gave me someone with the qualities God wanted me to have in a mate. This person came to be someone who I saw and spoke to daily and lived in the same apartment complex as I.

An eighteen-year veteran of the Tampa Police Department and eleven years my senior, he is a charming man of integrity, compassion for others, and humility. We first met when I moved in to my apartment. I was out washing my car and a truck pulled up beside me. The driver got out to rinse off his truck, or so I thought. He put out his hand to shake mine and introduced himself. We talked briefly and he left. At the time, he was dating someone else. About a year later, on my way home, I looked in the rearview mirror, and there he was, but in a new truck. As I got out of the car, he stopped me to show me the new truck he was driving. From that day on, he would stop when I saw him and talk to me. So one day, I went to the leasing office in the complex and told a woman there about him. She said he happened to work as a security officer for the complex. She ended up giving me his number, saying that we would make a good couple. I was already scared because I had never considered dating anyone eleven years my senior, but I thought I'd give him a try. Plus, what did I have to lose? I would probably gain a good friend in the process. However, it took me three days to call. Supposedly, they let him know I had the number, so I believe he was waiting. I prayed about it and then called. We talked on the phone for about a month before taking it further. He asked me out twice and I turned him down, because I wasn't ready to date yet. Finally, I called him and asked if he would go out to the movies with me. We have been together ever since. It was truly God–sent. After five months of dating, he proposed. A week later, on August 31, 2001, we married. In November, he was promoted to sergeant. The next April, on my birthday, we closed on our beautiful home, one that God led me to. Then God's ultimate blessing came—one that I thought I could never physically do. On July 1, 2003, at 7:07 a.m., I gave birth to a beautiful baby girl; she was three pounds and five ounces. God's promises are amazing! Nothing compares to God's love!

UNCOVERED AND NOT ASHAMED

The beginning of my marriage was truly heavenly bliss. I felt like no one could compare to my husband and that I was the best he could ever want or need from a wife. We had some glorious times. We took plenty of trips together and loved to just be in love. We felt we were the life of every party. Eight months after we got married, we moved into a new home. It was a house that I never thought I would come across. I was just passing by one day on my way home from work and saw a brand new development of homes being built. When I stopped by, I had this overwhelming feeling of excitement. I asked the sales rep to please show me the model, and the rest was history. I took my husband back to the model and we were both so incredibly thrilled that we *had* to take a step of faith and get that house. It had not been built yet, so we were able to choose everything from the paint to the tile, and even what fixtures we wanted. So we built from the ground up our brand new home. He did a special surprise and closed on my birthday, flowers in one hand, and the keys to our home in the other. We were so excited. And immediately upon moving in, we started having gatherings. We loved to be social and inviting to people. Everyone could tell of our happiness and we openly loved to share it with others. Romance completely filled the air on a daily basis and we did everything we could to show each other how much we adored one another. The only difficulty we had was agreeing to come together as one on matters that dealt with the Lord. For the Bible says in Amos 3:3, "Can two walk together, except they be agreed?" Even though I believe he loved the Lord, I felt that many of the things that I was accustomed to doing before I got married—paying tithes and offering, going to church almost four nights a week, being in ministry with singing—were compromised, because I thought that once we married, he would also do those things. It didn't happen the way I thought. So one thing I learned and want to share with you is this: If the person you are trying to get to know is not already doing those things that please God and you know constitute a mate who has a heart for God, don't think they will do those things once you are married to them. They have to be already convicted and practicing those things as a single person before meeting you. Even though those things were a red flag for me, I still loved him for the man that he was and didn't want to try to change him.

About a year and a half into our marriage, we became pregnant. I considered it a wonderful time for me, especially considering the doctors before told me that I may never be able to get pregnant during my first marriage. God knows exactly what he's doing and when he wants to do it; we have to be patient and wait on him! If he said it, that settles it! So we started making plans for our new baby by putting together the baby room, buying car seats and furniture, and child-proofing the house. I thought the pregnancy went extremely well, but what I didn't know was I had a condition that is not uncommon in many women; I had pre-eclampsia. It is a condition where all of a sudden your blood pressure goes up extremely high and causes you to have to have the baby much earlier than expected. It also caused me to look much bigger as a pregnant woman by gaining greater levels of water weight. By the time I reached my eighth month, my 120-pound frame went up to 174 pounds, mostly from water. One could tell that because if you were to pinch or push my skin down, it would have left the fingerprint still there. I was that way over my whole body. My feet and ankles were swollen, my nose spread, and my fingers looked as if they were unable to close into a fist. My husband noticed it one night while lying down and became extremely concerned and told me to go into the doctor the next Monday. My appointment wasn't until that following Friday, but I listened to him and said that I would go in. Well, my baby shower was that Saturday before, so we left our cares behind for that moment and enjoyed the fellowship of friends and family. But that Monday, when I walked into the doctor's office, after taking a couple of routine tests I normally would do every time I went in, the doctor immediately told me to head for the hospital. At 160/100, my blood pressure was extremely high, and if I didn't get it down quickly, I could have had a stroke. Crying as I left the doctor's office, I immediately called my husband and told him to meet me there. Minutes were long waiting for him to show up. I became frightened by all of the commotion that was going on. Nurses were on both sides of me trying to find a vein to start an IV to no avail. Finally after forty-five minutes, things settled and I was officially admitted into the hospital and a somewhat comfortable bed. But my pressure became higher and higher. The doctor came in and said the baby must be taken now. I had no chance to give a natural birth and it really upset me. I thought to myself, *My baby is going to be premature the same way I was.* But I figured it's better to have a premature baby than one with possibly worse complications. So we went ahead with the C-section. July 1, 2003, my daughter was born weighing only three pounds, five ounces. My husband and I didn't even know she was taken over to the incubator because I asked him to continue talking to me throughout the surgery so I wouldn't be nervous. She was so quiet and didn't cry one bit. But after the surgery, I ended up with a blood transfusion. So much blood was lost because the doctor thought the incision was not completely sown properly and had to redo it. All this time, I didn't know where I was or what was going on. I couldn't see my daughter to really begin the bonding process for three whole days. I felt miserable because I wanted to be there with her. But I knew God had everything under control. Today, you wouldn't be able to tell that my daughter was a premature baby. She is happy, healthy, and thriving even more so than her classmates and little friends. She is my joy and a ray of light every morning, especially Saturdays, as she taps me on the shoulder to wake me up and need something. I love her dearly and thank God for her every day.

But even with all of what God was doing in our lives, which I believe was truly God's favor, the devil knew just what our weaknesses were and what to do to bring those to the forefront. Never could I have imagined my life being glorious and loving one minute, with my world unfolding upside down in the next. The devil truly knows how to be busy in my business.

THE DEVIL SURE KNOWS HOW TO BE BUSY IN MY BUSINESS

After about nineteen days, my daughter was brought home from the hospital. She was a small and quiet little baby who didn't cry much unless she was hungry or needed to be changed. Because of how small she was, it was really frightening to me since I was a first-time mom. But I did what I thought was best. My husband already had two children from previous relationships, so he had a hand in the baby changing, feeding, and caring for. But instead of it making me feel better, I started to envy it. I felt like he knew everything and how to tell me what to do and how to do it.

Since he worked at the time during the day, I was at home and felt like the walls were caving in. I hated being at home and longed to be back at work. Each passing day at home seemed like an eternity. There was not enough shopping at the mall, going to the grocery store, or running errands that would keep me from wanting to go back to work. This created a feeling of neglect and isolation from my baby. I didn't know what it was at the time, but I would remember holding my baby many days while in a rocking chair, not even looking at her. I was so tired and felt so big. For months, my relationship sexually with my husband was at a standstill. Ever since I learned of me being pregnant, our lovemaking stopped. Maybe he felt that he would hurt the baby. Many men do, so I hear. So the feeling of inadequacy and not really being wanted crept in. The only solace that I felt at that time was to pamper myself. How? By shopping, mostly online, but when I felt like being seen in public, I would go to the mall or anywhere to spend money. Over a six-month period, I'm sure I spent close to $3,000 in clothes alone. And I didn't feel bad about it. The only thing I felt was confusion as to why none of my new clothes fit me. I was buying sizes I wished to get back into. It was sad. I wanted my husband to understand, support, and encourage me and treat me like the wife I knew I was. But instead, he became angry of my spending habits. I began to feel like I was being dictated to on issues dealing with the baby. I felt like a child with no sense of responsibility. I ended up with a serious case of postpartum depression. Everything made me sad. I had crying outbursts, wanted to sleep all of the time, and was very emotional. This was just the tip of the iceberg for us, and slowly things began to dwindle.

As the first year of my daughter's life began to go by, it became time to celebrate her birthday. I'm usually big on planning events and looked forward to celebrating my daughter's big day in grand style. So about two weeks in advance, I sent out invitations and made a few calls. Never did I think I would have a problem getting kids and friends of the family to show up. July 1 came and, to all of our surprise, only four people showed up to sing happy birthday and give grand wishes to our baby girl. I felt awful, but what made things get even more out of hand was the argument that ensued as people left the event. Again, I didn't do a good job, so I thought. My husband ranted and raved on the number of people that arrived and why I hadn't planned this out sooner. Suddenly, the comment that I never thought I'd hear left his mouth: "If I have to do everything around here, I don't need a wife." A hush fell across the house. All I could do was count to ten. Instead of using that time to really think about what I would say, I resorted to biting back and said, "Okay, since that's how you feel, I won't be a wife anymore." I then started to do things for my baby and myself only. If he came home expecting dinner, dinner would be there, but only enough for me. She would have been fed baby food, and we would be full and well-rested. Our clothes would be washed, but not his. I was fed up and tired. I felt I did all I could do for him. My needs, physically and emotionally, were not met. I thought about and did things that only pleased me. I also started to look for others who would validate me and make me feel special. Many of them were men I would talk to on the phone, just to vent and have someone to console me during what I thought was a stressful time. But I didn't even fathom going further than that. The devil seemed to know the right time to spring into action to take control of the one thing that he finds you to be weak in. He will crank up the volume on your life and put that weakness right in front of you just to tempt you to take that plunge that ultimately can change or turn your life upside down. And never will it be the same.

Communication was completely broken after this point in time. We couldn't seem to get anything that was pressing out in the right manner without one of us breaking down or getting on the defense. Many nights we would be in bed together, but never touching each other, and hardly saying goodnight. All this time, I was still talking to other people about my problems, but never telling the one person I needed to about them—God himself. I felt like I had to go to all others to help me work it out, or to have people tell me I was worthy and deserving of attention and pampering by my husband. But why wasn't this being communicated to my husband? Now that I look back, I realize how and why many of my relationships failed; they had so much to do with my childhood and the abandonment and neglect I felt. I hated rejection; I felt this very same way with my husband and wanted to find someone who would give me attention and companionship, even if over the phone.

As time went on and other encounters became more apparent with people of the opposite sex, I ended up succumbing to the temptation to step outside of my marriage. Somehow with all of the negative effects post–partum depression had on me already with my baby, and the inadequacy I felt, it left me no other choice than to only think of myself and my self–fulfillment. I not only wanted to feel the warmth and affection that I so longed for by my husband, but I wanted to feel like me again—free to love, laugh, and feel sexy in my own skin. I started to see myself going out more, getting things that at one time I thought women shouldn't have, like a tattoo and belly–button piercing, but now they made me feel more complete as a person. Whether it was right or wrong by society's norms didn't matter anymore.

Six months after stepping out, I finally decided to tell my husband the truth. Now mind you, all of this time that passed made me more and more cognizant of my wrongdoing, and all of my close girlfriends and mom told me, "Don't do it. If I were you, I'd go to my grave before I'd tell him I messed up." And I really should have listened. However, I had a deep burning of guilt inside of me and have always been raised to do the right thing. So I felt I had to get it off of my chest to keep from feeling the guilt that would ensue. But for many other people, it was a way to feel better about myself for telling him, not thinking about the upcoming effects of the pain he was getting ready to feel.

January 2, 2005, I finally sat him down after a day at church to tell him the one thing that would change both of our lives forever. I think when I first shared it with him, he didn't believe what was coming out of my mouth because he did a double take. However, when it finally settled in that I cheated, his once calm, soothing, and peaceful face immediately turned to disgust and anger—a face I never thought I'd see. From that day to more than a year later, ours lives were a living nightmare. We fussed and argued every night, questions pertaining to my affair lashed out over and over for me to relive every second that transpired, and all I could do was cry, get defensive, and cry some more. I wanted it to stop already. I figured by telling him, all I was saying was that I had had enough and wanted to walk away from it all. My mind was not on my child then, even though I know I was taking good care of her, so I thought. But for some reason, he had to know more. The devil was extremely busy and happy for the entire trauma this act caused our once loving family. People on the outside looking in thought they saw a great couple who just gave birth to a beautiful baby. They saw us in a new home and living life to the fullest. But what they failed to see was the lack of communication that created a barrier on what we needed to know from one another to keep us together in the first place. We both had high expectations for the other and wanted so much instead of just being satisfied with what we both had and building upon it to make our marriage grow. I can't say we were ever friends before we started our love together. I do feel friendship is and should be the foundation in every relationship because you already know what makes that person tick and what he or she likes and dislikes, and you can talk to one another about anything. With those things, trust and understanding are built. But we had the opposite; friendship and trust were never fully established.

We continued on this downward spiral for a whole year, trying to find ways to make the marriage work. But I'll admit, it was extremely hard. I couldn't go out without him questioning me, checking my phone, and asking what time I was to be home. If a show on television came on that had anything to do with extramarital affairs, it opened up a whole can of worms for another argument. The times of once sitting down with each other and talking out our problems became an all out fighting match with pushing and shoving and an occasional hit or two. It became so bad that the last straw came when my daughter, around two and a half years old then, came to me when I was crying one day and asked, "Are you okay Mommy? Did daddy hit you?" I knew then, it was time to leave. I didn't feel like being a wife anymore; the love I once had for him vanished, and it was time to call it quits.

Even though our marriage didn't last the way we truly hoped it would, we are more cordial now than I think we ever were. We listen to each other in a way I never thought we could and express ourselves on a much deeper level when it comes to caring for our daughter. It seemed that it took my daughter some time to get used to having two households, but I've got to say she was a tough cookie. She acted very mature for her age and has turned out to be a happy, well–adjusted little girl. Even though we didn't work out, I can say that my ex–husband is a wonderful father and a good man. We will always care for each other and want nothing more than to see the best for both of us. I feel that all of the trials and tribulations I've been through with past relationships are continually teaching me things about myself. It has shown me to just be *me;* I don't have to settle or fit into some-

THE LIFE OF A LILY

one else's mold. If I just display who I am from the onset, in all of its splendor, either one of two things will happen: Either the other party will run away, or he will see me for the woman that I am and who God made me to be and know that this is a person to get to know. Either way, I'm better for it. I thank God for the experiences. And I thank my ex–husband for the time we shared.

FALLEN BUT NOT DEFEATED

My brother has always been known as "Reece Cup," or his stage name, "Po Child Cup." Growing up was somewhat trying in my family—definitely for him and me because we never really had the chance to grow up together. We knew we were siblings, and we would hang out every chance we got, but it was only hours at a time. He is my only brother on my biological mother's side of the family. Because of my being adopted by my grandparents, we were split up. He stayed with my mom, while my grandparents cared for me. I have distinct memories of my childhood with my brother. We would do many crazy things. There were times when my great–grandmother was living where she would be asleep in her rocking chair. We would sneak up to her and step on her foot and run. We would swing on the trees in the front yard, tear down branches, make mud pies, and get all dirty. I would end up being the one getting in trouble for what we did. He would even chase me down the street to catch me and take me back to my grandmother for me to get the beating he should have received. I remember him laughing at me while I sat and cried after being whipped. Then we would fist fight because I would be so mad at him for laughing. When my brother and I were away from each other, it was then when I began to learn a lot about my brother and how he and my mother had to survive together. Being a single parent was hard, I'm sure. One thing I can say about my biological mom was that she had to be strong, a lot like my grandmother was. Moving from place to place with a child was difficult in itself. He grew up sheltered and protected by my mother. Other times he tried to play man of the house, making it difficult for my mother to get into different relationships with men. My brother never really saw the good in any man that wanted to date my mom. He would even get into fights with them and eventually get his way of having mom all to himself.

My brother was pretty well taken care of. My mom may not have been rich or anything, but the money that was brought in all went to him: clothes, jewelry, sneakers to match every outfit, extraordinary "Gumby" haircuts (the style of the Nineties), and money in his pocket. He was perceived to be a man even before he was of adult age. All the girls loved him and other men wished they could be like him. The only issue my brother had was his temper. I think all of our personalities left much to be desired when it came to our temperaments. We all had crazy ways of dealing with our anger, but his took the cake. He definitely had a quick temper, and do not look at him wrong, let alone talk about him, his mother, or his sister.

As time went on, my brother got himself into some illegal activity that also stirred up his desire for alcohol and illegal drugs. The devil knows how to play on one's emotions and uses those emotions to enhance his own devices. The Bible says, "Lest Satan should get an advantage of us: for we are not ignorant of his devices" (2 Corinthians 2:11). Because of that, we have to remember what Peter told us: "Be sober, be vigilant; because your adversary the devil, as a roaring lion, walketh about, seeking whom he may devour…" (1 Peter 5:8). So when my brother engaged in these drugs, it caused his anger to increase. Many things people would normally do for fun would cause him to spiral out of control in anger and frustration, as if people were out to get him. The anger would spur out to family members, his close friends, and us. In Ephesians 4:26–27, it says, "Be ye angry and sin not: let not the sun go down upon your wrath: Neither give place to the devil." It's hard for so many people to realize that it's okay to be angry so long as you don't take that anger and use it against someone to provoke or incur sin. Many people wanted to and did turn their backs on my brother, maybe in fear, or maybe because others were feeling rejected because they loved him so much. So many personal relationships were lost. Soon the drugs and alcohol turned into actually pushing these drugs on the street. Of course, he felt that this was the best way to make ends meet with his six children to take care of. Was he the best father and provider? Maybe; maybe not. Nonetheless, he loved each and every one of them the same. He had a long-term relationship with a young lady who fell deeply in love with him and ended up conceiving four of his six beautiful children. He would hit the street, hustling with other fellows who really didn't have his best interest at heart, but they didn't make too much mention of it, for fear of his retaliation. Regardless of his actions and how he chose to live his life, I still had such love for him as my little brother. And he made sure to let everyone know that I was his big sister, even to those who never really knew we were related. Oh, but when they found out, they looked at me so differently, as if to say to others, "Don't mess with Reece's sister. You know he doesn't play." One thing I can truly say about my brother, however, is that he knew the Lord Jesus Christ. He made an attempt every day to read the Word, and he would talk to you about what he read. He knew how to call on the Lord, and he always seemed interested in Jesus' Word.

He always had talks with little kids, especially the ones closest to him, about doing the right thing, even if he didn't. That meant to me that maybe he didn't want others to do some of the things he was doing; he wanted others to be better.

Family was always a priority to him, and I started to understand this during one day that ultimately changed my life. On Sunday, November 6, 2005, I had decided to get up one morning with my daughter and travel to Kissimmee to see my mom. I wasn't going to go that day, but instead go to church; however, my mind changed and I decided to get on the road. So once I got there, shortly after arriving to my mom's home, my mom and I decided to go and see my nieces and nephews around the corner because my brother didn't live very far from my mom's house. On our way to his place, my mom told me to drive down a certain street to see if we saw him. When we turned onto that street, we saw him leaning on a garbage can in front of a house he always hung out at to hustle and make a few dollars for his family. I don't condone what he did; I even told him to get a job for his family. All of his family repeatedly said this, but to no avail; he made the decision to continue what he wanted to do. We stopped where he was and talked for a minute. Then he said he needed to go to the dollar store to pick up some things for the house, so we said we would take him. It had been a long time since I had the chance to be with my brother and mom together. While in the store, we joked, talked, and laughed about the number of children he had and the fact that I didn't need anymore because he had enough to go around for all of us. He laughed it off like he always would and kept shopping. We left there and went to a corner store to pick up some drinks, then made our way back to his place. We helped him get his groceries in the house and then he escorted me back to the car. Then it seemed like everything went in slow motion. As I was getting back in the car, he stared me in the face and said, "I love you big sis." I said, "I love you too." We kissed each other, and then he left, going back to the street and the house he was hanging out at when we came to get him earlier that day. That was the last time I saw him and had the chance to say "I love you." Days went by and things started happening to me that I never really caught and paid attention to until it was too late. One day that week, while I was lying in bed trying to sleep, I felt something so heavy upon me that I felt the enemy himself had overtaken me. I felt the sense of death and dying all over my body, hovering over me. I was frozen. I started praying right there in my bed. At first, I thought it had a lot to do with what I was watching on television and the shootings in Iraq, the hurricanes in Louisiana and Mississippi, the recent tsunami and the overwhelming death tolls that occurred with each of those events. Immediately the next day, I told a good friend of mine what I experienced. We immediately went into prayer, breaking down strongholds like never before. I didn't know for whom I was praying, but I prayed anyhow. It will get like that sometimes. God will send you important warnings and messages through your dreams. It is important to recognize what God is trying to relay and go into intercessory prayer.

> Likewise the Spirit also helpeth our infirmities: for we know not what we should pray for as we ought: but the Spirit itself maketh intercession for us with groanings which cannot be uttered. And he searcheth the hearts knoweth what is the mind of the Spirit, because he maketh intercession for the saints according to the will of God.
>
> Romans 8:26–27

As I went through the rest of the day, the heavy burden was lifted. But then other things started happening. Shortly thereafter, I received two significant e-mails. The first e-mail asked for everyone to send the e-mail to their loved ones, telling each person that you love him or her, for tomorrow may not be promised to you, and for those people, who do not have e-mail, call them and tell them that you love them. So of course, I sent the e-mail to as many people as I could. The next e-mail I received, told a story about a girl named Tammy. The story was about how Tammy would get into many difficult situations, and each time she prayed to God asking to help her. Every time, God fulfilled his promises and healed her, fed her, paid her bills that were overdue, and delivered her family. She would praise God, but then say, "Oh, I still have time. I'll wait to get saved when I'm thirty. As her thirtieth birthday was approaching, she had a birthday party and invited everyone she knew. But unfortunately, she didn't make it to her thirtieth birthday. At 11:59 p.m. on the day before her birthday, she passed away. I was amazed and shaken by this e-mail. Then I had a dream that still has me thinking, even today. The dream was about my brother and me. We were standing on the same street he was on that past Sunday. On this street, I was talking with him about getting his life together, getting a job, and raising his family. For some odd reason, my brother wasn't himself. In the dream, it seemed he was under the influence of something because all of a sudden, he became enraged and started cursing obscenities at me. I knew right then it was time for me to leave. As I started taking off running down the street toward my mother's house, he tried to grab me. I got loose and ran with him not far behind me. As I was turning around to see where he was, I noticed he had something in his hand—possibly a gun. I finally approached my mom's house, went inside, took my baby, and started for the car. My mom, in all the uproar, came from her room, asking what's wrong. I told her, "I'm sorry Momma, but I've got to go. I can't come back here anymore."

She said, "Why? What happened?"

I said, "Momma, Reece is behind me in a rage. He's going to hurt me if I don't leave." So I got in the car with my baby. As I started the engine and started to back the car up, I looked up, and there he was with his fist coming through the windshield, and I woke up. Later, I would realize how much these e-mails and my dreams were trying to prepare me for what lay ahead. God has a way of giving signs of warning to you; it's your job to pick up on them and go into prayer.

Thursday, November 10, 2005, was a day of more signs and wonders that my family started to recognize as my brother's final day. I had been working very hard as a teacher all school year, trying hard not to take any days off, trying to build up some time for sick leave and such. My fellow co-workers knew of my hard work and told me that I should take a day just to relax because if I did, I would end up having a four-day weekend because Veteran's Day was that Friday, November 11. So with some thought, I decided to take the day off. I did my normal day of relaxation—slept in, watched television, and considered myself blessed to be off that day. It wasn't until one o'clock in the morning on the eleventh that I felt selfish for thinking I could rest when someone very close to me had to fight for his life. As I was asleep in bed, I received a phone call. When I picked it up, I heard my mother's voice. She was rather calm, but I knew something had to be wrong when calling that late. All I remember hearing her say was that my brother was dead. I immediately sat up in the bed, saying, "What?" She said, "They have killed my boy. They got what they wanted." All kinds of emotions ran through my mind, and all I could say was, "No, no, no he's not. Momma, what happened?" In her seemingly calm voice, she started to tell me what seemed to replay in my head over and over again for several weeks thereafter.

Earlier that day, my mom went to see him to tell him how her day went at her job. It was the last day she was to be at her job because she was hired at another hotel with benefits and she was so excited because her former hotel gave her a going away party to say goodbye. At about six o'clock that evening, she stopped where he normally hangs out and called him to her car so she could tell him. They talked a little bit. She noticed he was kind of down, not himself. She asked if he was all right.

He said, "Yes, ma'am. I'm all right." He kept hanging on to the car as if he wanted to go with her but she felt that if he said he was all right, then he was all right.

So, she said, "you be easy, okay?"

He said, "okay, baby." And she went on to her house. Supposedly, sometime between six and ten o'clock that night, a confrontation ensued between my brother and a few people, one being a girl that he knew and her boyfriend, his brother, and another one of their friends. The girl played a key part in what happened next because she is the sister of a guy who my brother had a confrontation with about two years ago, and, in self–defense, my brother shot her brother in the foot. In the process of the incident, one of my brother's ex–girlfriends, was shot in the arm by the crossfire. My brother did some jail time for that; however, charges were not brought against him. God set him free. I thought after that he would be ready to change his life for the better.

This girl held a grudge for two years. Her intentions from the start were to get back at him for what he did to her brother. When they came up in the car, they exchanged words and then they left. During this time, my brother felt a little uneasy and had decided to go to his house to get his gun. But an older man that my brother knew very well convinced him, in so many words, that getting a gun was not the answer, so he stayed where he was until a little after eleven o'clock that night. Meanwhile, back at my mom's house, my stepfather woke up out of his sleep, saying to my mom that he needed to go to the store. I do believe to this day that God woke him up to witness my brother's demise. After going to the store on his scooter, he decided to ride down the street to see if Reece was down there. He found Reece sitting in the dark in front of the house he normally hangs out at. Two other boys were standing at the road in front of the house when my stepfather pulled up. He said he talked with my brother for about two minutes before a car pulled up, but he noticed the car's headlights were turned off. My stepfather told Reece that he was going to go home and get some sleep. As he was going to get back on the scooter and ride away, two guys got out of the car. My stepfather noticed the same girl that was there earlier with them was driving the car. Another guy was also in the car waiting. When the two guys got out of the car, one of them started yelling obscenities, asking, "Where's that punk that was running his mouth?" Of course, my brother didn't back down from anyone and would call himself out if he had to. So he stood up from his chair and went toward them. All the while, my stepfather was standing between them in the road. All of a sudden, my stepfather said he froze. He looked down in one of the guy's pockets and noticed the barrel of a nine–millimeter handgun hanging out. He yelled, "They got a gun." Immediately, my brother put his hands up and backed away from the guys, as if to say, "Man I don't want beef with you, I don't have a piece." As he turned around to take off running, one of the guys started yelling obscenities again, and everyone, including the two guys who were hanging out at the road before the car pulled up, scattered—everyone except my stepfather; he couldn't move. The guy fired a shot one time in my brother's back. It went straight through him. He cat walked, running with his hands, trying not to fall down. He continued running through the bushes behind a house. There was a struggle with the two boys who had the gun when one of them tried to take the gun from the other who started shooting to shoot some more. He shot three more times, but missed everyone. They got back in the car and sped off. My stepfather was left there to witness it all. Reality set back in and he started looking for my brother with his scooter through the bushes he saw him run in. He called out his name as loud as he could but heard no answer. So he went back to the house and called my mom out of her sleep to tell her that my brother had been shot. She woke up in a crazed state and started out in the car looking for him. His girlfriend was also at the house asleep, so she went with my mom. All of them started traveling down the street he was on, going from street to street. Then it seemed God said to my mom, "Go down this street." As she got closer to our community church, she saw in a back alley behind the church what looked like a body lying in the road. Sure enough, there was my brother in a pool of blood. He had been trying to run to my mom's house. He was only about two yards away from my mom's front door, in the alleyway. I can imagine he felt, "If I could just get to my momma's house, I'll be all right." He ran a good two blocks before collapsing to the ground. When she found him, his eyes were set and gray, blood had formed between his teeth, and he had released himself; he was already gone.

After mom told me the story over the phone, I started thinking back over the week's events that happened to me and realized God showed me what was ahead. I then started thinking to myself, *Lord, when he was running and trying to get away, did he call on the name of Jesus?* Then scripture started coming to me.

> That if thou shalt confess with thy mouth the Lord Jesus, and shalt believe in thine heart that God hath raised him from the dead, thou shalt be saved…For the scripture saith, whosoever believeth on him shall not be ashamed…For whosoever shall call upon the name of the Lord shall be saved.
>
> Romans 10:9, 11, 13

I also remember times when I have prayed with long suffering for my family, including my brother. While I was reading a book by Judy Jacobs, called *Take It by Force,* I ran across a scripture that was in her book: "For from the first day…your words were heard" (Daniel 10:12, NAS). Now I understand when the Bible declares, "Believe on the Lord Jesus Christ, and you will be saved, you and your household" (Acts 16:31).

I pray daily for the salvation of the people that acted in hatred for my brother and shot him senselessly. I pray that they ask for forgiveness and remember that the Lord said, "It is mine to avenge; I will repay" (Romans 12:19). Jesus said,

> And I say unto you my friends, Be not afraid of them that kill the body,
>
> and after that have no more that they can do. But I will for warn you whom
>
> ye shall fear: Fear him, which after he hath killed hath power to cast into hell;
>
> yea, I say unto you, fear him.
>
> Luke 12:4–5

Since then, one of the boys had been placed in jail, but it was not the one who actually shot and killed him; it was his brother taking the rap for him. Can you believe that? It's amazing how the devil can truly take over your mind to do evil and hateful things to other people. He spent ten months in jail. At the trial, none of the witnesses that were present at the time of my brother's murder would come forth. Only my stepfather testified. Because there was not enough evidence to convict him, he walked away a free man. That may be the case now, but the Lord will ultimately judge.

It is time for us as a people to call out to God in times of trouble, not your own devices. God is omnipotent and omniscient. He can do what we ourselves cannot. I had to learn this the hard way. Soon after my brother's death, I started having panic attacks, headaches, constant fatigue, and trouble eating and sleeping. The passing of my brother was pretty rough on me. I couldn't do anything but call out to God for deliverance and protection for me and my family and go into complete warfare over the devil. Even now, when the devil wants to rise up against me, whether on my job, in my family members, or whatever, I'm reminded that "God has not given me the spirit of fear; but of power, and of love, and a sound mind" (2 Timothy 1:7). The Bible also says, "Thou wilt keep him in perfect peace, whose mind is stayed on thee: because he trusteth in thee" (Isaiah 26:3). I'm going to keep everything under the submission of the Lord, including my mind. I have decided that no weapon formed against me or my family is going to prosper.

I've come to see that this was all in God's plan and that he never makes a mistake. Of course I miss my brother, but I also know he's in a better place—a much better place. And when we meet again, in heaven, we will shout and celebrate, because Christ will prevail! Hallelujah!

WHEN YOU THINK ALL IS SAID AND DONE, LOOK WHAT GOD CAN DO

There have been and will continue to be many more experiences and trials in my life; it's truly just a matter of growing from all of them and making sure I present myself as a finer woman, mother, daughter, and child of God to the best of my ability. Maintaining relationships with all I associate with can be a rewarding experience or a difficult task. However, I must remember where I came from and what it took me to get here. That will keep me grounded and more mature to encounter all that lies ahead.

I've recently come into contact again with my biological father. My half–sister called me to tell me someone wanted to speak to me, and when I heard his voice, tears just started to stream down my face. I felt like a little girl again, but this time I didn't harbor any negative feelings towards him. We talked for a few minutes to realize a few things: he has diabetes and an enlarged heart. It tore me up inside to hear, and I felt so much compassion for this man. But it also woke me up about my own heart murmur and my health in general. My biological mother has heart problems also, so this was important to know. Now is our relationship the greatest? No it's not. Our relationship is not the greatest, as I still have difficulties daily with opening my heart and letting him come in. It's something I'm steadily working on. I'm hoping and praying that God will speak to both of our hearts and allow us to fully restore our relationship before it's too late. Another sad thing that I found out was that my favorite aunt on my father's side, whom everyone has said I took after and looked like, died four years ago from cancer, and no one had told me. I hadn't seen her in years and she had been fighting cancer for ten years. She was almost sixty years old. All I could do was cry. I then took

Bible that God does not distinguish which sins are bigger than others; a sin is a sin! Lying is just as great as murder or stealing. We cannot judge one another. "For all have sinned and come short of the glory of God" (Romans 3:23). I just want him to come out from under his bondage and ask for forgiveness, get into a church, and get a job and live where he doesn't have to hustle the way my brother did. God can bring a miraculous change in anyone's life. It's evident in so many people I know. And he can do it for you, too!

I hope that all who have read this book have grown if but a little bit from the experiences I've gone through. I hope that if you have been through things like these, you realize that God still has you here and has a plan for you, for a reason only God can show you. He may have shown you while reading this book. Continue to keep your head up, knowing that whatever situation you are in or have been in happened for your good! It may have been rough, and it may have been hard to get your head above water, but there's sunshine on the other side. I had to learn this, too. Thank you, Jesus! I pray that you, too, will see the salvation of the Lord. I am not where I want to be—I haven't arrived—but I am also not where I used to be. But I am striving daily for his perfection and excellence. And because I am a child of God, I now have the opportunity to do just that! God Bless!

> Lord, I thank you for giving me the opportunity to share my life with other people around the world. I pray that you would renew their minds, blow your spirit within them, and bring the Shechinah Glory upon them like never before. I pray that every burden that was on their shoulders be lifted right now in the name of Jesus. You know their needs, wants, and desires. The devil has been trying to play with their minds and hearts for too long, thinking that you are not for them or with them. But you said you would "never leave them, nor forsake them" (Joshua 1:5). Bring them to a kind of intimacy like none other, knowing that you love them and want to see nothing but the best for them. In the name of Jesus, I now proclaim that the past is the past and that they have victory! I love you! In the mighty name of Jesus, thank you and amen!